Dedicated to the memory,
and the humor,
of Barbara Shafer and Ryan Shafer.

CONTENTS

INTRODUCTION

THE BOTTOM LINES are what count most with many readers of the *Wall Street Journal*'s widely read Friday page-one column, the Washington Wire. At the end of the column is where you find those funny one-liners called "Minor Memos" that capture the weekly humor of Washington. And here, for the first time, is a collection of the best of the Minor Memos—from Bill Clinton and Bob Dole to the Nixon days of Watergate. The humor is sometimes hysterical, often historical—jokes of the day trace the rise and fall of President Jimmy Carter, for instance—and frequently stands the test of time. Every good comedian knows that a funny line never dies; it just gets recycled for another day.

The Washington Wire is a grand tradition at the *Wall Street Journal*. The column was started in 1940 by its first writer, Barney Kilgore, who went on to build the *Wall Street Journal* into the nation's largest newspaper. The inside-Washington column was given its name by Bill Kerby, who later succeeded Kilgore as chairman of Dow Jones & Co., which publishes the *Journal*. For thirty years until late 1984, the wire was written by Washington features editor Edward Behr, who perfected its compact writing style. Ronald G. Shafer began as Ed's backup wire writer in 1977. In late 1984, he and feature editor Rich Jaroslovsky took over the column. One of

Minor Memos

The Wacky Side of Politics and Power from the *Wall Street Journal*'s Washington Wire

Compiled by Ronald G. Shafer

Andrews and McMeel
A Universal Press Syndicate Company
Kansas City

 For information write to Andrews and McMeel, a Universal Press Syndicate Company, 4520 Main Street, Kansas City, Missouri 64111.

Library of Congress Cataloging-in-Publication Data

Minor Memos: The Wacky Side of Politics and Power from the *Wall Street Journal*'s Washington Wire / compiled by Ronald G. Shafer.

p. cm.

ISBN 0-8362-2756-5 (pbk.)

1. United States—Politics and government—Humor. I. Shafer, Ronald G.

PN6231.P6S76 1997

320.973'0207—dc20 96-33999 CIP

Book design and composition by Top Dog Design

their goals: to focus even more on finding those funny Minor Memos. In 1994, Ron Shafer assumed primary responsibility for the Washington Wire and for the Minor Memos.

The Washington Wire, however, is not the creation of any one writer. As the column's heading states, the wire is "A Special Weekly Report From the *Wall Street Journal*'s Capital Bureau." The material is reported and submitted by reporters in the *Journal*'s Washington bureau, under the leadership of Washington Bureau Chief Alan Murray, Deputy Bureau Chief Jill Abramson, and Chief Political Reporter Jerry Seib. But it is all those Washington politicians, bureaucrats, jokesters, and movers and shakers who have the final funny words—intentional or not—that we call "Minor Memos."

CHAPTER ONE

See How They Run

IS THIS THE NEW HAMPSHIRE STOP?

Asked by tourists how to get to the White House, a Washington subway attendant says, "First, you enter the primaries."

• • • • • • • • • • • • • • • • • • • •

STANDING SMALL

Four-foot, eleven-inch Barbara Mikulski, senator from Maryland, says she can't run in New Hampshire's presidential primary because "I can't figure out how to be seen above the snowdrifts."

• • • • • • • • • • • • • • • • • • • •

GETTING THE BIRD

Humorist Bob Orben says, "Thanksgiving is when you get to live with a turkey for weeks; elections are when you get to live with a turkey for years."

THE OLDER GUY THING

Signs seen at a Bob Dole rally in St. Louis:
"Real women love Dole."

••••••••••••••••••••

WIFE TO WIFE

When asked his position on presidential debates, presidential challenger Bob Dole responds:
"I think Elizabeth ought to debate Hillary."

••••••••••••••••••••

LEFT BEHIND?

When President Clinton shakes hands after a speech in Royal Oak, Michigan, a woman gives him a suit—size 46 long.

SWAN SONG?

An informal poll by the Mr. Showbiz site on the Internet asked what should replace the Bob Dole campaign's former theme song "Dole Man." Top choices: "Livin' on a Prayer" and "Slip Slidin' Away."

• •

DOLE OVERBOARD!

Looking for help? Dole plans a campaign stop in Hampton, N.J., at the Switlik Parachute Co., which makes inflatable life rafts.

• •

READ MY SLIPS

Comedian Bob Somerby says Bob Dole's campaign flaps are reestablishing his reputation as "The Grating Communicator."

DRIVE-BY FISHING

Comic presidential candidate Pat Paulsen declares his stand on gun control: "As a sportsman, I've always felt guns should only be used for fishing."

••••••••••••••••••••••

HAVE A SEAT, PLEASE

Comedian Mark Russell on the GOP's gentler image: "A nice conservative is someone who advocates upholstered electric chairs."

••••••••••••••••••••••

GIVE THIS MAN A JOB

Retired General Colin Powell introduces himself as "former soldier, former author, and now unemployed nonpolitician."

FAMILY VALUE

Comedian Kevin Nealon, reporting from the 1996 Republican Convention on Jay Leno's show, says affluent Republicans have their own version of Hillary Clinton's book: "It Takes a Nanny."

CONVENTION WISDOM

Comic Jenny Church on GOP convention security: Conservatives, wary of moderates, installed "middle detectors."

WRONG HAIR DAY

"Mr. Kemp, can we take your picture?" a teenager asked a silver-haired man at the 1996 GOP convention in San Diego. "Sure," said Connecticut Senator Chris Dodd, "but I'm a Democrat."

HERE'S THE DEAL

After Ross Perot said he was interested in his Reform Party's presidential nomination, some say he has a new theme song: "It's My Party, and I'll Run If I Want To."

••••••••••••••••••••

UNMADE AT ANY SPEED

Green Party presidential candidate Ralph Nader contends Bill Clinton's mantra is, "A mind is a terrible thing to make up."

••••••••••••••••••••

STUMPED SPEECH

Presidential candidate Bob Dole, asked by a reporter the most important quality he would like voters to know about himself, replies, "Beats me."

NOBODY FOR CONGRESS

Playing off the slogan "Nobody in Washington cares about you," Joe Magee in Alabama asks that his nickname, "Nobody," appear on the GOP ballot for Congress.

•••••••••••••••••••••

ANYBODY FOR CONGRESS

Walter Mondale relates that in campaigning for the Democratic representative from Texas, Jack Brooks, he asked the first person he approached in Brooks's district if he would please vote for Jack Brooks for Congress. The man replied, "I sure will. We've got to get rid of the guy who's in there."

•••••••••••••••••••••

FAINT PRAISE

A GOP newsletter calls Chic Hecht, senator from Nevada, "a man whose accomplishments are unknown even to many in Washington."

READ MY HIPS

Looking toward Clinton's reelection campaign, the Capitol Steps comedy troupe has an Elvis-like President Clinton singing "Return to Center."

• •

DON'T BE CRUEL

A sign in the office of Clinton campaign official Ann Lewis reads "It's the Incumbency, Stupid."

• •

ALL SHOOK UP

A perplexed child in Sandoval, Illinois, stares at Bill Clinton and asks his mother, "So where's Elvis?"

• •

SOUR NOTE

The National Taxpayers Union unveils the "Ballad of Veto Bill," a "taxin' politician who can never get his fill."

AT LEAST IT WASN'T A FLOWERS SHOP

Democratic presidential candidate Bill Clinton visited a factory that makes cheesecakes.

•••••••••••••••••••

BEAR MARKET

Washington jokes about three new government bonds—the Clinton bond has no principle, the Dole bond has no interest, and the Gingrich bond has no maturity.

•••••••••••••••••••

DOLEFUL BOB

U.S. Ambassador to Japan Walter Mondale says Bob Dole, his vice presidential opponent in 1976, "should be beatable. Even I beat him."

ON THE MAP

Comedian Mark Russell says that in a name recognition poll in California "most people thought Mondale was a small town near Pasadena."

••••••••••••••••••••

HOW COLD WAS HE?

Al Gore says it was so cold in Washington this winter that people were "huddling around Bob Dole for warmth."

••••••••••••••••••••

DUTY CALLS

GOP presidential candidate Bob Dole tells voters in South Dakota: "You don't have to like me, but you ought to vote for me anyway."

YOUNG BOB

To counter the age issue, seventy-two-year-old Bob Dole tells New Hampshire voters he has thought of running with Senator Strom Thurmond: "He's ninety-three, and it would balance the ticket."

• •

FRUIT OF THE GLOOM

A Washington bumper sticker:
"Dole isn't even a good banana."

• •

DOLE ON WRY

Bob Dole, recalling George Bush's tendency in campaign travels to claim the states where Bush ancestors lived as his own, quips: "I hired a genealogist, and we now have thirty-two home states; they're all the early primary states."

TRANSFUSION ALLUSION

Dole, noting that his wife, Elizabeth, is president of the Red Cross, says, "At least she's president of something, which is more than I can say."

• • • • • • • • • • • • • • • • • • • •

MY THREE POLS

Bob Dole in 1980 on Jimmy Carter, Ted Kennedy, and Jerry Brown: "As I look at the three Democratic candidates," he says, "I hear a drawl from the present, a voice from the past, and a beep-beep-beep from the future."

• • • • • • • • • • • • • • • • • • • •

FLAG WAIVER

A GOP pledge of allegiance by the Gross National Product comedy group ends with "one nation, under Dole, invisible, with no liberal justices at all."

CAPITOL PUNISHMENT

After his loss in the Louisiana caucuses, some say Senator Phil Gramm's presidential campaign is being made into a new movie: *Dead Man Walking*.

••••••••••••••••••••

HOW BIG IS IT?

The Republican senator from Michigan, Spencer Abraham, joking about Steve Forbes's wealth, says Lamar Alexander "walks across New Hampshire; Forbes takes about the same time to cross his own lawn."

••••••••••••••••••••

STANDING PAT

Patrick Buchanan says that if he runs for president, his campaign slogan will be "Why not the Beast?"

IN YOUR HEART YOU KNOW HE'S FAR RIGHT

Political humorist Mark Katz says Pat Buchanan's first draft of his convention speech reads, "Extremism in the defense of extremism is no vice."

••••••••••••••••••••••

MY DOG DAN

The New Hampshire chairman of Pat Buchanan's 1992 presidential campaign calls Vice President Quayle "the pit puppy for the Bush administration."

••••••••••••••••••••••

HERE'S THE DUO

Comedian Mark Russell dismisses a third-party pairing of Colin Powell and Ross Perot because "you don't balance a ticket with a general and an emperor."

TANKS FOR THE MEMORIES

Jay Leno proposes a presidential bumper sticker for General Colin Powell: "I look better in a tank than Dukakis."

• •

NOT ALREADY!

The day after the 1996 presidential election, a bumper sticker appears in Boston with the trademark Lamar Alexander plaid and a simple "2000."

WE HAVE OVERCOME

"Republicans suddenly are up in arms against affirmative action," says political humorist Mark Katz, "now that the Democrats are a minority."

PHIL DOES DALLAS

Senator Phil Gramm's blast against Senator Bob Dole's "kiss your sister" tax-cut compromise prompts a retort after reports that Gramm once invested in an in-law's R-rated movie. Dole aides chuckle that *Kiss Your Sister* is the title of the latest Gramm-financed movie.

•••••••••••••••••••••

IN THE DARK

Washington disc jockey Jack Diamond jokes that Gramm invested only $5 in a porn flick, "but he didn't think anybody saw him go in."

•••••••••••••••••••••

GOING TO EXTREMES

Offering to help counter political attacks, the media firm of Creative Response Concepts sends letters to one hundred GOP lawmakers that begin "Dear Mean-Spirited, Radical Extremist."

OH, BABY!

The governor of Wisconsin, Tommy Thompson, introducing presidential candidate George Bush at a Waukesha County GOP dinner, roars, "It's time for the Bush pregnancy to begin!"

•••••••••••••••••••••

ECONOMIC GROWTH IS HELL!

A New Jersey union official, introducing George Bush as the hero of Desert Storm, says the president is now poised to "declare war on the economy."

•••••••••••••••••••••

MIDNIGHT MIKE

Republicans joke that it isn't true that Democratic presidential challenger Michael Dukakis doesn't have a defense policy; being from Massachusetts, it is "one if by land and two if by sea."

BALD CHARGE

GOP Senator Alan Simpson charges that Dukakis's defense position "has more loose ends than a $10 hairpiece."

• •

GOOD OLE DUKE

Michael Dukakis's running mate Senator Lloyd Bentsen quips that the Democrats failed to carry Texas because "I just wasn't able to convince the voters that Dukakis was Greek for 'Bubba.'"

• •

HE'S THE ONE

A T-shirt with a picture of vigorous-looking Richard Nixon and the message: "He's tan, he's rested, he's ready for 1988."

• •

CHARISMATICALLY CHALLENGED

One fellow conservative gibes at Paul Trible, senator from Virginia, as "Richard Nixon without the charm."

ANATOMICALLY INCORRECT

Democratic presidential candidate Jerry Brown refers to campaign cash as "the umbilical cord that . . . every major politician in this country still sucks on."

••••••••••••••••••••••

BOGEYMAN

The governor of California, George Deukmejian, says golf and politics are different—in politics "you can't improve your lie."

••••••••••••••••••••••

YOU D'MAN!

Al D'Amato, senator from New York, is greeted at a campaign visit to a senior-citizens center by a sign reading "D'Feat D'Amato."

STANDING STUCK

Texas agriculture chief Jim Hightower says that in politics the definition of status quo is "the mess we're in."

••••••••••••••••••••

OY VEY!

Prescott Bush had to destroy nineteen thousand letters seeking money to help pay off debts from his aborted campaign for the Connecticut Senate nomination; all were mistakenly addressed "Dear Rabbi."

••••••••••••••••••••

PRESIDENT PIERRE

Democratic pollster Harrison Hickman, in an interview with *Public Opinion* magazine, says of the presidential prospects of Republican Pierre du Pont: "When you have the first name of a maitre d' in a French restaurant and a last name that invokes toxic waste, you have a problem."

A LEG UP

Comic Jenny Church says that in order to be seen as a leader, Ross Perot is changing his group's name to "United We Stand on an Orange Crate."

• • • • • • • • • • • • • • • • • • • •

LOCK AND LOAD

A sign spotted along the Ronald Reagan campaign trail: "Pass the Lord, Praise the ammunition."

FIGHTING WORDS

A sign by anti-Reagan demonstrators at a Republican rally read "Give War a Chance."

• • • • • • • • • • • • • • • • • • • •

WAY BACK IN THE SADDLE

Walter Mondale solemnly told a California audience of a discovery that could affect the election: "In Reagan's first movie, Gabby Hayes got the girl."

ALL WET

Democrats adopt a slogan mocking Reaganomics: "Don't trickle down on me."

••••••••••••••••••••

ALL POLITICS IS LOCAL

A Santa Barbara, California, magazine puts President-elect Reagan's picture on the cover with the caption "Local Rancher Makes Good."

••••••••••••••••••••

JUST SAY FIRST LADY

Humorist Robert Orben says: "Governor Reagan will bring to the White House determination, resolution, and a will of iron. But enough about Nancy—let's talk about Ron."

PUMPING HISTORY

After Walter Mondale picks Geraldine Ferraro as his running mate, a San Francisco shoestore quickly advertises women's pumps with the sign "Shoes for a Vice President."

•••••••••••••••••••••

SHE DOES!

A sign seen at a vice presidential candidate Geraldine Ferraro campaign appearance in Memphis: "God loves an uppity woman."

•••••••••••••••••••••

BEHIND EVERY WOMAN

Looking back, Francis O'Brien, who served as Geraldine Ferraro's press secretary, says he would do one thing differently: "I wouldn't iron her dresses anymore."

THIRD-MAN THEME

The Democratic Party, an official says, will try to keep Independent candidate Representative John Anderson off presidential ballots using means both "legal and political."

••••••••••••••••••••

HEEERE'S JOHNNY

Johnny Carson tells an NBC affiliates' gathering that Independent presidential candidate, white-thatched John Anderson, is the perfect counter to Ronald Reagan: "He's young with old hair."

••••••••••••••••••••

RAPID RESPONSE

Oklahoma Democratic Senate candidate Jim Boren promises to get back to callers "as soon as possible. If you're calling about a campaign contribution, I'll get back even faster."

READ MY GROVEL

After Bob Dole announced he would quit the Senate, Wisconsin Governor Tommy Thompson's office faxed GOP publicists a statement praising the "bold and courageous move," adding: "Is this enough?"

••••••••••••••••••••

HONEST, ABE!

Michigan Senator Spencer Abraham talks of joining Florida Representative Lincoln Dias-Balart for a future GOP White House bid as the "Abraham-Lincoln ticket."

••••••••••••••••••••

BIG CHEESE

A political tale: A new children's book on Congress is called "House Mouse, Senate Mouse," featuring "the squeaker of the House."

HELLO, DALI

In honor of the 1996 presidential debates, the Salvador Dali Museum in St. Petersburg, Florida, invited the media to a reception called "Experience the Surreal."

• • • • • • • • • • • • • • • • • • • •

FOUR PLAY

Presidential candidate Bob Dole tells a campaign crowd: "Here are two four-letter words you can teach your kids: Dole-Kemp."

• • • • • • • • • • • • • • • • • • • •

LAST HURRAH

"I don't think about being president any more," Senator Ted Kennedy tells a union conference. "I don't think about it any less either."

CHAPTER TWO

Only in Washington

TRADING PLACES

Tommy Downs, imprisoned for fraud involving student loans, tells senators: "The possibility of one of you gentlemen being in my position is probably greater than the other way around."

•••••••••••••••••••••

A BILLION HERE, A BILLION THERE

Comptroller General Charles A. Bowsher says that "statistically, the difference between $45 billion and $50 billion is insignificant."

•••••••••••••••••••••

TO TELL THE TRUTH

A candid panhandler near the Capitol carries a sign that reads "Hell, why lie? I need a beer."

COFFEE, TEA, OR FILIBUSTER?

On an airline flight stopping at Washington, a flight attendant asks if passengers will be going farther or getting off at "Hot-Air Haven."

• •

AS YOU WEREN'T

The answer: Shannon Faulkner, who dropped out of the Citadel a few weeks after becoming the first woman to enter the all-male military university.

The question: Who has more military experience than Bill Clinton and Newt Gingrich combined?

• •

BACKSEAT WHINER

Twitting House Speaker Newt Gingrich's complaints about being seated in the back of Clinton's plane, Democrats suggest nominating him for "chief petty officer of Air Force One."

THE BEAT GOES ON

Congressman Sonny and no Cher: The line between satire and actual events was crossed, says comedian Mark Russell, "the day that Sonny Bono became a member of the House Judiciary Committee."

••••••••••••••••••••

HALF WITS

The *Washington Wit* tabloid announces a political action committee, WitPAC, to make donations to "candidates who say or do funny things, whether intentionally or not."

••••••••••••••••••••

DUCKING RESPONSIBILITY

Asked how he was preparing for testimony to Congress on the Clinton health plan, director of the Congressional Budget Office Robert Reischauer said: "I'm standing in the kitchen and having my wife throw pots and pans at me."

PLANE TALK

After a small plane crashes on the White House lawn and the opening of the Denver airport is delayed for months, some people ask: "What's the difference between the new Denver airport and the White House?" *Answer:* "You can land a plane at the White House."

••••••••••••••••••••••

AMERICA'S MOST TICKED OFF

Seen at the Clinton White House: a mock list of top ten reasons for foes to vote against the anticrime bill, including "Will only make criminals mad."

••••••••••••••••••••••

TWO-FOR-ONE SALE

A counter-list of top ten "little known provisions" in Clinton's crime bill includes "Five-day waiting period to buy a Congressman."

TONGUE OF DOLE

Asked about Defense Secretary Caspar Weinberger's response to reports that the Pentagon nearly paid $600 for a toilet seat, Senator Bob Dole quips, "He hasn't taken a position on that."

••••••••••••••••••••

IT TAKES ONE

Senator Dole jokes that this week's decision on the air bag was easy for his wife, Transportation Secretary Elizabeth Dole: "She's married to one."

••••••••••••••••••••

END GAME

Senate Majority Leader Dole doesn't see a lame-duck session after the fall elections because "tax reform will be finished, the budget will be finished—and some senators will be finished."

HOW SOON THEY FORGET

Clinton Treasury Secretary Lloyd Bentsen tells of an elevator encounter: "You're Senator Bentsen," says a man. "Whatever happened to you?"

••••••••••••••••••••

HOLD THAT THOUGHT

The message on Brookings Institution real estate expert Anthony Downs's answering machine says he is "too busy thinking great thoughts to come to the phone right now."

••••••••••••••••••••

STOP THE PRESSES

Federal Communications Commission member Andrew Barrett, after an appeals court reverses an agency rule he pushed, remarks: "I was wrong, and that's something that self-important people in Washington like me usually don't admit."

EQUAL OPPORTUNITY

Acting U.S. Trade Representative Charlene Barshevsky on her former boss Mickey Kantor taking over at the Commerce Department: "It always does my heart good when men become secretaries."

••••••••••••••••••••••

POTOMAC LOBBYISTS

Retiring Nevada Senator Paul Laxalt joins the parade of politicians into the capital's law firms by noting, "There are 4,000 lawyers in Washington, but if you needed a will drafted, you'd have to go out of town."

••••••••••••••••••••••

INSULT TO INJURY

Leaving court to meet reporters after pleading guilty to mail fraud, former House Ways and Means Chairman Dan Rostenkowski asks lawyers, "Are we goofy enough to stand in the rain?" The reply: "We have to."

DEAD POLITICOS SOCIETY

The four blurbs on the back of former House Speaker Jim Wright's 1996 book are quotes from deceased Presidents Kennedy, Johnson, and Nixon and the late Speaker Tip O'Neill.

• •

ROCKIN' RENO

Attorney General Janet Reno dances barefoot to "Mustang Sally" at a Justice Department holiday party.

• •

LET US PREY

When children attending a Washington church Christmas service were asked, "And what do we call men who watch after sheep?" an adult voice from the audience whispered: "Majority whips."

DIVINE GUIDANCE

Bush White House Chief of Staff James Baker, finding aide David Gergen talking to reporters at a military chapel service in Korea, admonished, "No leaking in church."

• •

AIR SUNUNU

After criticism that he used the White House plane too often, Bush Chief of Staff John Sununu, arriving late at a Washington fund-raiser, explains, "I couldn't find a place to land."

• •

TAKE MY REGULATOR–PLEASE!

A guard stopped Federal Trade Commission member Elizabeth Dole from entering a male-only San Francisco club but relented when her escort said, "This is no lady, this is a commissioner."

HIGH ANXIETY

Reagan Treasury Secretary Donald Regan praises the arrival of spring in Washington: "The squirrels are searching for nuts—which has a lot of Washingtonians nervous."

••••••••••••••••••••

BUCK PASSER

Treasury Secretary Regan, the man who signs the dollar bills, keeps on his desk a sign that reads "The buck starts here."

••••••••••••••••••••

WELCOME HOME

Jeane Kirkpatrick says that, as United Nations ambassador, "I'd be met by people chanting and wearing death masks, and that was just the White House staff."

CHAPTER THREE

Politicians Say the Darndest Things

OH, SAY, CAN YOU SEE?

At hearings on White House handling of FBI files, Senator Ted Kennedy condemns "rampart" speculation.

••••••••••••••••••••

CALL MY BROKER

In an SEC report on his stock trading, New York Republican Senator Alphonse D'Amato says his broker calls him "Uncle Al" and he calls the broker "Big Guy."

••••••••••••••••••••

IT TAKES A PILLAGE

Former House Speaker Tom Foley reveals the advice he gave Speaker Newt Gingrich on how to run the House: "Try not to rape and pillage too much."

ONE ON ONE

Senate Judiciary Chairman Orrin Hatch begins a speech with his top ten list of real courtroom lawyer questions, such as: "Were you alone or by yourself?"

••••••••••••••••••••••

BLAST FROM THE PAST

Back in the 1980s, Senator Bob Dole claimed that Jack Kemp favored tax reform in order to get a $1,000 exemption for hair spray.

••••••••••••••••••••••

GHOST RIDER

Senator Bob Dole said he wouldn't read Jack Kemp's new book "until I know who wrote it."

SOUL PERSON

A gender-neutral wordsmith, Don Riegle, senator from Michigan, tells Federal Reserve Chairman Alan Greenspan: "These are times that try men's souls and women's souls."

••••••••••••••••••••

PARTY ON

Frank Annunzio, representative from Illinois, tells *Chicago* magazine that he isn't worried about his district being redrawn because "the only thing that the federal law on redistricting provides is that the district be congruous and gregarious."

••••••••••••••••••••

ON THE STREET THAT I OWN

Senator Jay Rockefeller says he grew up playing with blocks just like everyone else: "Yours said A, B, and C. Mine said 49th Street, 50th Street, and 51st Street."

FAST LEARNER

At a hearing on education, Dale Bumpers, senator from Arkansas, praises his English teacher for giving him self-esteem, but concedes: "Some people think she overdid it."

•••••••••••••••••••••

WHO'S THE FOURTH ONE, DIRTY HARRY?

Republican Senator Max Baucus of Montana says: "Three out of every four Americans want strong clean air."

•••••••••••••••••••••

TERMS OF NO ENDEARMENT

Senator Alan Simpson of Wyoming jokes about people who "jump up and say, 'You deserve two terms—one in Congress and one in prison.'"

NOSE JOB

A press release for GOP Representative Nick Smith of Michigan says that by trying to preserve federal rules for Amtrak, "labor interests may be cutting off their nose despite their face."

••••••••••••••••••••••

I GOT MINE, BABE

GOP Representative Sonny Bono, lamenting bashing of the rich, says, "Nobody handed me anything. I don't think I have to share it with anyone. I did it, and it's mine."

••••••••••••••••••••••

EXCHANGE RATE

During debate on the House balanced-budget resolution, Representative Jim Lightfoot of Iowa declared, "If BS was a dollar a pound, we would have paid off the deficit at about noon."

MIX THAT METAPHOR

Senator John Warner of Virginia defends a highway-bill compromise by explaining: "You get in the only available lifeboat and stay aloft."

••••••••••••••••••••

SAY WHAT?

Senator Jim Sasser of Tennessee says of tough budget choices: "We have to belly up to the buzz saw, and I think we're reaping the whirlwind from it."

••••••••••••••••••••

HARD TO SWALLOW

Representative Henry Hyde of Illinois warns colleagues that special-interest groups will "go through the roof and climb down your throat—which, when you stop to think about it, is no small trick."

HOLY...ER, SMOKE

Representative Frank Guarini of New Jersey complains at a budget hearing that spending on federal benefits programs is growing "at an excremental rate."

••••••••••••••••••••

SKEWED AGAIN

Responding to Census Bureau remarks that the 1990 minority head counts are "skewed," Representative Gary Ackerman of New York declares: "Those people have been skewed since the beginning of the Republic, and they're getting skewed worse."

••••••••••••••••••••

NOT-TOO-FREE MARKET

Florida's representative Richard Kelly says, "I think that the free-enterprise system is absolutely too important to be left to the voluntary action of the marketplace."

GET OUT

Misreading the word "succeed" in his inaugural address, Governor William Clements declares: "The people of Texas want us to secede."

•••••••••••••••••••••

BEEPERS

Noting the ambitions of many of her colleagues, Senator Nancy Kassebaum suggests a new bumper sticker for senators: "Honk if you're not running for president."

•••••••••••••••••••••

WEIGHT WATCHER

Asked about his successful effort to quit smoking, drug czar William Bennett says, "I'm not sure I'm a better man, but I'm a somewhat bigger man."

DOWN ON THE FARM

Representative Pat Roberts of Kansas says the politically correct term for farmers and ranchers is "agro-Americans."

• •

POLITICALLY CHALLENGED

The Democratic National Committee adopts a new euphemism to refer to handicapped people: the "differently abled."

• •

SENATE STRESS

After hearing Senate testimony that mental-hospital workers need time off from their difficult work surroundings, Senator Pete Wilson of California remarks: "I can appreciate that. I work in a similar environment."

STAYING ALIVE

Representative Clair Burgener of California, speaking at an energy hearing, said, "Let me turn to California and get parochial. If I do not get parochial, the people will find someone who will."

••••••••••••••••••••

VIA THE HOLLAND TUNNEL

Trying to rally support for a proposal to have the government buy vans to transport employees, Representative John Burton of California began: "Van pooling is not a Dutch diplomat."

••••••••••••••••••••

MR. ED

A Dallas businessman, unhappy with the ad hoc House Energy Committee's bill, urged his congressman to "defeat Ed Hock's energy committee proposal."

JANITOR IN CHIEF

Asked who at the 1990 budget summit would be courageous enough to propose new taxes, Senator Bob Dole replies: "Maybe the custodian."

••••••••••••••••••••

UP CLOSE IS TOO PERSONAL

Senate Majority Leader Bob Dole, asked by colleagues if it was better to watch a Senate debate on C-Span as he had done, replies: "It is better because you are farther away."

••••••••••••••••••••

EYE ON NEWT

Senate Majority Leader Dole, skeptical of his House colleague's tax-cut push, warns of "the Gingrich that stole Christmas."

WHO'S MISSING?

Senator Lloyd Bentsen of Texas says, "There are ninety-nine prima donnas in the U.S. Senate."

• •

ELECTION TO GRAVE

GOP Representative Lawrence Coughlin of Pennsylvania, opposing an appropriation for a congressional cemetery, warned: "People are going to say, 'well, they finally found a way to take care of themselves from election to resurrection.'"

• •

THE INSIDE SKINNY

Representative Edward Markey says he plans to go on "the Wall Street diet: You lose it all in one day."

BLOCK THAT METAPHOR

House Speaker Jim Wright declares that "our society has created a casino of new financial techniques that may be putting us on a collision course toward economic Armageddon."

••••••••••••••••••••

HORSE OF A DIFFERENT STRIPE

Senator Al Gore, blasting President Bush for trying to appear proenvironment with his Grand Canyon trip, declared on the Senate floor that "a zebra cannot change its spots."

••••••••••••••••••••

ONE WOMAN, ONE VOTE

Ann Richards, Texas state treasurer, tells of a feminist sign of the times. One woman declared: "I'm really not political; I just vote the woman, not the party."

BOTTLED UP

Democratic Representative Pete Stark claims Republicans don't mind cutting the budget for clean water because they "drink and bathe in Perrier."

• •

TERMS LIMIT

House Social Security Subcommittee Chairman Andy Jacobs advises witnesses that "they will be allowed no more than two 'finallys' and one 'in conclusion.'"

• •

RED FACED

Senator William Armstrong of Colorado declines to yield to Senator Wyche Fowler during a debate because the Georgian is "so skilled in debate . . . he might embarrass me." Fowler's reply: "The senator is correct."

DRINKING BOOTS

Chairman of the House Armed Services committee Les Aspin said he's heard of parents sending "Jim Beam equipment" to their kids in the Saudi desert. He meant "L.L. Bean."

•••••••••••••••••••••

BY THE NUMBERS

Prosecutor Rudolph Giuliani of Manhattan, asked if he wants to be FBI director, attorney general, senator, or governor, replies: "No, no, maybe, maybe"—then says, "Did I get the order right?"

•••••••••••••••••••••

WHAT ARE THEY NOW?

A press release from Senator Jeff Bingaman of New Mexico talks of benefits that went to "over 400 former people."

WHEN WILL IT ALL END?

GOP Senator Steve Symms complains that public financing of Senate elections would keep Democrats in control "on and on, ad infinitum into the near future."

••••••••••••••••••••

ADJECTIVE OBSERVER

After Senator Max Baucus of Montana heaps praise on Treasury Secretary–designate Lloyd Bentsen at his confirmation hearing, Senator Bill Bradley of New Jersey remarks: "I'd like to associate myself with all of the adjectives that Senator Baucus used."

••••••••••••••••••••

BLOWING IN THE WIND

Representative Bob Michel jokes, "I support an air bag in every car. Unless a senator is on board, in which case it becomes redundant."

THOU SHALT NOT APPEAL

Representative Tommy Robinson of Arkansas says the Supreme Court "could find a loophole in the Ten Commandments."

••••••••••••••••••••

COALS TO NEW CASTLE

Celebrity divorce lawyer Raoul Felder attended Senate hearings, explaining that his specialty is "lies and deceit."

••••••••••••••••••••

NYET!

Senate Majority Leader George Mitchell's advice to visiting Supreme Soviet members on drawing up rules for their legislature: "Don't copy ours."

••••••••••••••••••••

FALL OUT

Presiding over the Senate, John Glenn, a former Marine combat pilot, crisply announces that the Senate will recess until "0830 hours."

CAJUN CHAOS

Chairman of the House Budget committee Jim Jones, in a Louisiana speech, gibed: "Word gets out that there's a Louisiana politician with a conscience and it may wreck the whole system down here."

• •

ON THE FRITZ

Democratic Senator Fritz Hollings asks: "How many White House aides does it take to change a light bulb?" His answer: "None. They like to work in the dark."

• •

OLD-TIME RELIGION

House Speaker Tip O'Neill, gibing at President Reagan's drive for school prayer, says, "He's a typical Republican—likes to save souls on Sunday and God help the poor on Monday."

ELUSIVE QUARTERBACKS

House Speaker Tip O'Neill says that immobilizing the MX missile by putting it in a fixed silo "would be like playing Doug Flutie in the pocket."

••••••••••••••••••••

REVOLTING THOUGHT

During the Nicaragua Contra aid fight, House GOP leader Bob Michel inadvertently refers to Central American nations as "the banana Republicans."

••••••••••••••••••••

HOG WILD

Representative Sherwood Boehlert of New York, the head of a water-projects subcommittee, threatens to police potential pork-barrel proposals with a project inspector general, or PIG.

••••••••••••••••••••

GROANER OF THE DAY

GOP Representative Joe Skeen, on why Congress blocked a federal labeling rule that distinguishes between "hard chill" and "fresh" chickens: "It needed more thaw-t."

••••••••••••••••••••••

PASS THE CRAYONS

Asked by the *Hill* newspaper what book he would suggest that new lawmakers read, Representative Thomas Bliley of Virginia says *All I Really Need to Know I Learned in Kindergarten.*

CHAPTER FOUR

Hail to the Chiefs

CLINTON HEALTH REFORM

The acronym for the Health Care Financing Administration, HCFA, is now said to stand for Hillary Can Fix Anything.

••••••••••••••••••••••

ASK NOT WHAT I CAN DO

The number one reason President Clinton chose Martha's Vineyard for his vacation, according to a popular T-shirt on the island: "He thinks he's a Kennedy."

••••••••••••••••••••••

NOT TO MENTION THE SNAKES!

Shaking hands at the Springdale, Arkansas, airport, President Clinton is tickled by a well-wisher's T-shirt featuring a picture of Socks and the inscription: "The mice in Little Rock are nothing compared to the rats in D.C."

ONE-STOP DIPLOMACY

Some Democrats refer to President Clinton's address in Haiti as the "I Shall Not Return Speech."

••••••••••••••••••••••

SHARK BAIT?

Asked what he wants to do on an upcoming trip to Australia, President Clinton replies: "Play golf with Greg Norman."

••••••••••••••••••••••

WHITE HOUSE LINKS

Former Vice President Dan Quayle marvels at President Clinton's ability to find leisure time: "He plays more golf than I do."

BUSHSPEAK

In a phone call to shuttle astronauts who had just launched a new space probe, President Bush asks: "But look, how was the actual deployment thing?"

••••••••••••••••••••

CROSS YOUR HEART

Commenting on the coming summit with Russian leader Mikhail Gorbachev, President Bush cautions, "I don't want to see over-promise coming from it."

••••••••••••••••••••

BUSHSPEAK LIVES!

The president says he mightn't have provided aid to Saddam Hussein before the Gulf War "if I had 90–90 hindsight."

••••••••••••••••••••

TERMINATOR TOT

President Bush describes meeting Arnold Schwarzenegger's infant daughter: "I bent over to kiss her and she tried to bench-press me."

THE DENY THING

President Bush, told that some people think he's too nice in dealing with Congress, retorts: "It's a terrible attack. I refute that."

• • • • • • • • • • • • • • • • • • • •

CANINE ADVICE

Campaigning for a New York congressional candidate, President Bush says, "Let me give you a little serious political inside advice. One single word. Puppies. Worth ten points."

• • • • • • • • • • • • • • • • • • • •

OUT ON A LIMB

President Bush assures police officers, "Our entire administration opposes chaos and lawlessness."

SAY NOTHING

President Bush describes a photo session at which he makes remarks but won't answer reporters' queries as "a modified limited photo op cum statement sans questions."

••••••••••••••••••••

GOOD KNIGHT

Former president Bush says that after Queen Elizabeth gave him an honorary knighthood, Barbara greeted him at home with the words, "Sir George, how about making some coffee?"

••••••••••••••••••••

CROSSING THE COLONIES

President Reagan joked to a group of senior citizens: "Just to show you how youthful I am, I intend to campaign in all thirteen states."

FELLOW TRAVELER

President Reagan tells a Florida audience that Ponce de Leon failed to find the fountain of youth: "I know. I was with him on the trip."

••••••••••••••••••••••

MY THREE STOOGES

President Reagan mistakenly referred to visiting Liberian leader Samuel Doe as "Chairman Moe." White House wags wondered if his chief aides are named Larry and Curly.

••••••••••••••••••••••

BOTH ENDS NOW

President Reagan got a big laugh, from both sides of the aisle, with this ad-lib in his speech to Canada's parliament: "If you will forgive me . . . you know someone once likened government to a baby. It is an alimentary canal with an appetite at one end and no sense of responsibility at the other."

SADDLE UP

President Reagan says his horseback riding confirms an old cavalry saying that "there is nothing so good for the inside of a man than the outside of a horse."

••••••••••••••••••••

ONCE EVERY SEVENTY-FIVE YEARS

Comedy writer Bob Orben jokes that President Reagan may be getting older but that there is no truth to the rumor he looked up at Halley's Comet and said, "Oh, there it is again."

••••••••••••••••••••

JIMMY, WE HARDLY KNEW YE!

A Southerner backing Georgia's Jimmy Carter rejoices: "For the first time, we have a presidential candidate without an accent."

MR. GOOD TEETH

Detroiters remarking on Democratic presidential candidate Jimmy Carter's appearance in the Motor City said he came in for his "30,000 smile checkup."

• •

ONE-MAN TEAM

A former adviser to another Democratic president jests that "Carter does the work of two men—Laurel and Hardy."

• •

HISTORIC HUMOR

A bit of black humor circulates at the Democratic National Committee: "What do George Washington, Thomas Jefferson, Abraham Lincoln, and President Jimmy Carter have in common?"

Answer: "None of them has done much for his country lately."

SINKING FEELING

Humorist Art Buchwald says, "I worship the very quicksand Jimmy Carter walks on."

••••••••••••••••••••

OUT OF GAS

Latest fuel-shortage joke—Every president since Herbert Hoover has promised to put two cars in every garage; Jimmy Carter is the first to succeed.

CHAPTER FIVE

We're Number Two— The Veeps

SERIOUSLY, FOLKS

Capitol Hill wags refer to the serious-minded Albert Gore as "prematurely grave."

••••••••••••••••••••

YAWN

"Al Gore is so boring that his Secret Service code name is—Al Gore." Who said so? Al Gore.

••••••••••••••••••••

ONE LITTER BOX AWAY

Vice President Al Gore, delivering a speech in a cast after his basketball injury, quips: "It takes me twice as long to walk Socks now."

••••••••••••••••••••

QUAYLE HUNTING

Wall Street traders describe Dan Quayle as the ultimate zero-coupon bond: "No maturity, no interest."

UP A CREEK

Vice President Quayle thinks Roe versus Wade are alternative ways to cross the Potomac River.

••••••••••••••••••••

CAN YOU SPELL POTATOE?

An instant collectible from the 1992 Republican convention: a button with a slash through a picture of Dan Quayle and the words "Just Say Noe."

••••••••••••••••••••

A CERTAIN MAYBE

Vice President Dan Quayle says, "I believe we are on an irreversible trend toward more freedom and democracy—but that could change."

THAT ABOUT COVERS IT

Quayle says he supports efforts "to limit the terms of members of Congress, especially members of the House and members of the Senate."

••••••••••••••••••••••

QUALIFIED CANDIDATE

James Boren, founder of the International Association of Professional Bureaucrats (INAPROBU), writes presidential candidates offering to serve as a running mate; one qualification cited: "I can profundify simplicity at the drop of an issue."

••••••••••••••••••••••

EARLY BUSHSPEAK

Vice President Bush promises to protect voters from "narced-up terrorist kind of guys."

IT WORKS FOR ME

Vice President Bush declares that his top goal will be to "make sure everybody who has a job wants a job."

••••••••••••••••••••••

A PERSPIRING EXAMPLE

Vice President Bush tells a Detroit audience that America's freedom is "the example to which the world expires."

••••••••••••••••••••••

UNPLUGGED

When the TV lights went out during an interview with foreign reporters, Walter Mondale quipped that one trouble with being vice president is that "from time to time you run short of power."

PLAYING SOFTBALL

At a Mondale press conference, a California TV reporter asks: "Would you care to comment on any developments anywhere in the world over the past 48 hours?"

••••••••••••••••••••

PARTISAN VIEW

Vice President Mondale offers his explanation of why Democrats outnumber Republicans: "We are more handsome, we are happier, we are warmer, we are sexier, and we have more kids."

••••••••••••••••••••

CHAPTER SIX

Bumper Snickers and Other Slogans

PRESS CLIPPING

A pro-GOP bumper sticker read, "Newt the Press."

• •

STILL THE ONE

A button says, "Nixon '96. Death is no excuse."

• •

ONE FOR THE AGES

A bumper sticker read, "Dole 96/Clinton 49."

• •

BOTTOM LINE

A bumper sticker declares, "Politicians and diapers should be changed often."

• •

CLINTONIZING

The advertising slogan of the Arkansas division of the American Cancer Society: "Be Like Bill. Don't Inhale."

WILLIE WONKA'S POLITICAL FACTORY

A bumper sticker seen in Washington during the Clinton administration says, "Wonk if you love policy."

••••••••••••••••••••

GRUMPY OLD MEN

A button seen in Washington reads, "Thurmond & Helms in '96. Don't Waste 200 Years of Experience."

••••••••••••••••••••

CLAWS OUT

A T-shirt lists the top ten reasons Clinton vacations at Martha's Vineyard, including, "The crabs are in the mud, not in the Senate."

••••••••••••••••••••

DUELING DISCIPLES

Democrat Mark Warner, hoping to unseat the GOP senator from Virginia, John Warner, issues a bumper sticker: "Mark, Not John."

OFF THE HOOK?

A bumper sticker on the Clinton administration and the Whitewater prosecutor Kenneth Starr says, "Don't Blame Me! I Cooperated with Ken Starr."

• • • • • • • • • • • • • • • • • • • •

ENDANGERED SPECIES?

Democratic Senator Dale Bumpers reports a bumper sticker in Arkansas that says, "To hell with the snail darters, save the Democrats."

• • • • • • • • • • • • • • • • • • • •

DESIGNATED DEM

A T-shirt for Democrats reads, "Friends don't let friends vote Republican."

• • • • • • • • • • • • • • • • • • • •

FREE WILLY

A T-shirt seen at the Conservative Political Action Conference: "Save the Males."

FIGHTING WORDS

Taking exception to the all-volunteer military, a bumper sticker seen in Washington reads, "Draft my ex-wife—Please!"

• • • • • • • • • • • • • • • • • • • •

LAMB CHOPS

A woolgrowers' association bumper sticker: "Eat More Lamb—50,000 Coyotes Can't Be Wrong."

• • • • • • • • • • • • • • • • • • • •

GOVERNMENT GODFATHER

A bumper sticker urges, "Fight Organized Crime—Abolish the IRS."

• • • • • • • • • • • • • • • • • • • •

BEAT THE PRESS

A bumper sticker at Bush-Quayle headquarters: "Annoy the Media: Reelect Bush."

BLAME GAME

New York Republicans distribute an all-purpose bumper sticker: "It's Mario Cuomo's fault."

••••••••••••••••••••••

BIG BAD BIRD

A bumper sticker protests Senator Larry Pressler's moves to cut public broadcasting: "Let's save PBS, privatize Pressler."

••••••••••••••••••••••

MOOD OF THE TIMES

A bumper sticker reads, "Know your enemies. They are your leaders."

••••••••••••••••••••••

ARE YOU THE SPEAKER?

"Question Authority," says a bumper sticker seen on Capitol Hill.

GLOWING REVIEW

A pronuclear bumper sticker reads, "Nuclear plants are built better than Jane Fonda."

••••••••••••••••••••••

WHAT'S UP, DOC?

Foes of nuclear power sport T-shirts that say, "The only safe breeder is a rabbit."

••••••••••••••••••••••

STILL CRAZY AFTER ALL THESE PROTESTS

A pronuclear power bumper sticker urges, "More nukes, less kooks."

••••••••••••••••••••••

MOBY JANE

A bumper sticker put out by a pronuclear group: "Feed Jane Fonda to the Whales."

MY FELLOW POSTAL PATRON

Senator Pete Wilson of California reports this bumper sticker: "Do something about junk mail. Tell your congressmen to stop sending it."

••••••••••••••••••••

CHOOSE YOUR WEAPONS

A T-shirt urges, "Make War, Not Love: It's Safer."

••••••••••••••••••••

COURT OF APPEAL

A T-shirt spotted in downtown Washington reads, "Real Men Marry Lawyers."

••••••••••••••••••••

FURRY FOOD

A protester's Reagan Inauguration Day sign: "Let 'em Eat Mink."

FIRST STEP

A bumper sticker after the resignation of Nixon's vice president Spiro Agnew: "One down, one to go."

CHAPTER SEVEN

Your Government Inaction

FREUDIAN SLIP?

At a White House briefing, Transportation Secretary Federico Pena praises the "White House Office of Environmental Apology."

••••••••••••••••••••

NOT-SO-BIG BROTHER

Peering over the microphones at an educators' conference, four-foot, ten-inch Labor Secretary Robert Reich inquires: "Do I look like big government to you?"

••••••••••••••••••••

THAT'S NOT AMORE

Outgoing Clinton staff chief Thomas McLarty, criticized for being too easygoing, says of successor Leon Panetta: "What this White House really needs is a chief of staff who can read Machiavelli in the original Italian."

HAMBURGER HELPER

Wendy's founder Dave Thomas says one way to pick up the pace at federal offices would be "to install straight-backed chairs."

•••••••••••••••••••••

PERMANENT EMPLOYEE

A sign in an office at the Council on Wage and Price Stability states: "A taxpayer is a person who doesn't have to pass a Civil Service examination to work for the government."

•••••••••••••••••••••

THOSE CRAZY TAXPAYERS

The Federal Communications Commission has employees view an instructional videotape on "Handling Psychotic Public Contact."

THE MAIL IS IN THE MAIL

Senator David Pryor demands a Postal Service apology after forty thousand pieces of 1992 Christmas mail to Arkansas and Tennessee were "discovered to have been misplaced for the past year."

•••••••••••••••••••••

SEARCH ME

U.S. intelligence agencies adopt a bureaucratic euphemism for what used to be known as "black bag jobs." The new phrase is "uncontested physical searches."

•••••••••••••••••••••

PROMISES, PROMISES

State Department spokesman Bernard Kalb opens the year's first daily press briefing by announcing a New Year's resolution "to be candid, frank, useful, and constructive." His response to the first question: "I have nothing that I can offer you on that."

CHECK THE LIBRARY

A private investigator extracts FBI documents under the Freedom of Information Act including a press clip quoting French philosopher Jean-Paul Sartre as promising to take an active part in the "Who Killed Kennedy Committee." FBI chief J. Edgar Hoover wrote at the bottom: "Find out who Sartre is."

••••••••••••••••••••••

JOB DESCRIPTION

Asked what he's looking for in a new Securities and Exchange Commission chief accountant, Chairman Richard Breeden responds: "A cross between Confucius, Superman, and Attila the Hun."

••••••••••••••••••••••

STANDING STILL

There's a new parlor game called "Bureaucracy." The first person who moves loses.

WHAT'D I SAY?

The Federal Energy Regulatory Commission issues "a notice of inquiry into the potential to interface incremental pricing and curtailment policy."

• • • • • • • • • • • • • • • • • • •

HOUSTON, WE HAVE A NEGATIVE SITUATION

Space jargon reaches new heights: A press release on the decision to let the Skylab space station fall toward Earth says, "NASA terminates Skylab reboost-deorbit activities."

• • • • • • • • • • • • • • • • • • •

GIVE ME SOME INTERFACE, MAN

An OSHA document on skin disease observes that "the skin is an important interface between man and the environment."

• • • • • • • • • • • • • • • • • • •

HOOTERS

An Interior Department press release refers to an "owl site center." What's that? A nest.

BOTH SIDES NOW

A senior Bush administration official, speaking on background about the National Security Strategy Report, says, "The main theme of this year's report is continuity and change."

•••••••••••••••••••••

WELL, EXCUSE ME!

A new guide to dining at the Pentagon discusses how to "maximize your Basic Urban Replenishment Period, or BURP."

•••••••••••••••••••••

MASSAGE CENTER

For NASA employees rubbed the wrong way by recent job cuts, this sign appears at the space agency's headquarters: "Massage Therapy Appointments Still Available."

STAND BY YOUR DAN

The National Center for State Courts, in a nod to an oft-maligned litigation critic, calls the GOP tort-reform bill "the Dan Quayle Revenge Act."

•••••••••••••••••••••

THE WAY IT IS?

Former CBS anchorman Walter Cronkite recalls that while covering the first manned trip to the moon he said, "If man can do that, we can do anything," and now complains that "man hasn't done a darn thing since then."

•••••••••••••••••••••

PERFECTLY MUDDY

Bush administration national security chief Brent Scowcroft dodges a question in a press briefing by saying: "That's a good question, and let me state the problem more clearly without going too deeply into the answer."

EITHER WAY

Asked at a House hearing about possible revision of the Consumer Price Index, Heath and Human Services Secretary Richard Schweiker replied: "Let me be explicit. This administration may be looking at across-the-board revision, or nonrevision, of the index."

•••••••••••••••••••••

IN YOUR HEART–OR YOUR TANK

A worrisome environmental hazard is leaking underground storage tanks—LUST for short.

•••••••••••••••••••••

FELINE INTRUDER

The Pentagon awards a contract for "interior intrusion detection systems"—better known as burglar alarms.

•••••••••••••••••••••

BUREAUCRATIC HANDLE

A Labor Department press release refers to truck drivers as "transport equipment operators."

IT WAS TESTED ON POSTAL WORKERS

A funding bill for the White House and the Treasury bars any employee training that "contains elements likely to induce high levels of emotional response or psychological stress in some participants."

••••••••••••••••••••

WHATTA TEAM!

A proposal to merge the House ethics and administration committees, says one Washington veteran, would be "like merging the League of Women Voters with the Los Angeles Raiders."

••••••••••••••••••••

NAME THAT BILL

Democratic Representative Henry Gonzalez introduces the Nonproliferation of Weapons of Mass Destruction and Regulatory Improvement Act.

I'M WALKIN'

The Postal Service bestows a new title on its plan to move some letter carriers from wheels to foot travel; it's "route demotorization."

• •

FISCAL PLUMBERS

Senator Fritz Hollings of South Carolina gibes that defenders of a budget accord are like "a drunk who stares at the leaky faucet and declares it fixed."

• •

IN OTHER WORDS, YOU PAY!

The Senate GOP proposes to "enhance graduate and professional students' responsibility for education expenses by removing government interest-rate subsidies."

TO DIE FOR

People for the Ethical Treatment of Animals asks the Federal Trade Commission to revise the fur-label term "animal producing the fur" to read "animal slaughtered for the fur."

••••••••••••••••••••••

NUCLEAR EUPHEMISM

Nuclear regulators propose "controlled purging of the environment" at Three Mile Island; they mean pumping poisonous gas into the air.

••••••••••••••••••••••

EROSION PROBLEM

The Treasury offers President Reagan a euphemism for tax increases: "tax-base erosion control."

••••••••••••••••••••••

NO KIDDING

The Census Bureau reports that two-thirds of urban poor people live in poverty areas.

CHAPTER EIGHT

Scandalgates: From Whitewater to Watergate

NO DOZ D'AMATO

The comedy troupe Gross National Product reports that "Sominex Corp. has successfully tested its first cure for insomniacs—the Whitewater hearings."

••••••••••••••••••••

CONSPIRACY HUMOR

Whose fingerprints were found on the document that mysteriously appeared next to Hillary Rodham Clinton's White House office? Oliver Stone's.

••••••••••••••••••••

REAL HARD COVER

The first lady is under so much fire, says comic Jenny Church, that her new book "doesn't need a dust jacket—it needs a flak jacket."

ON HER TOES

After the scandal breaks about Clinton adviser Dick Morris's affair with a call girl, a Democratic strategist suggests a title for Morris's book: "For Whom the Belle Told."

••••••••••••••••••••

OH, OLLIE

Forget about Hillary Rodham Clinton talking to Eleanor Roosevelt, says comedy writer Bob Orben, "I worry about politicians talking to Laurel and Hardy."

••••••••••••••••••••

LIDDY TO ELEANOR

Bob Dole remarks, "My wife is so talented that Eleanor Roosevelt is trying to reach *her*."

••••••••••••••••••••

THERE IS A FREE LUNCH

Observers suggest the congressional check-kiting scandal gives new meaning to the term "on the house."

CONSTITUTIONAL AMENDMENT

Ralph Nader calls the House bank flap "a scandal of checks and imbalances."

• •

WE TAKE NO CHECKS

Representative Bob Traxler of Michigan, who was robbed and beaten near the Capitol, now jokes that what really got his assailant mad "was when I offered to write a check."

• •

IRAN-GATE: In which the Reagan administration secretly traded arms to Iran for hostages, using the proceeds to finance clandestine aid to the Nicaraguan contra rebels through a network led by Reagan aide Lieutenant Colonel Oliver North.

• •

ASLEEP AT THE SNITCH?

Americans for Democratic Action sells $1 buttons that read "Did Reagan know or was he napping?"

SEE NO EVIL

Humorist Art Buchwald believes President Reagan's claims of ignorance: "After six years, why should he know something now?"

•••••••••••••••••••••

HO, HO, HO

Humorist Dick Flavin offers appropriate Christmas carols: "We Caught Ronnie Playing Santa Claus."

•••••••••••••••••••••

WAKE ME WHEN IT'S OVER

The Iranian crisis, one joke goes, is causing Reagan a lot of sleepless afternoons.

•••••••••••••••••••••

HEADS OFF

The difference between Iran and the United States in the Iran-Contra flap, one wit says, is that "when Iran's Khomeini says heads will roll, that's really what he means."

STILL RUNNING

Queried about whether the Iran scandal might make the 1988 GOP nomination not worth having, Senator Bob Dole responds quickly: "I'll take it."

•••••••••••••••••••••

OLLIE'S SONG

The Capitol Steps comedy group has a new song: "Thank God I'm a Contra Boy."

•••••••••••••••••••••

PERFECTLY CLEAR

Vice President Bush, attempting to explain whether he or President Reagan believed that arms were being traded to Iran to free the hostages, tells reporters: "I know what I know is what he knows . . . I don't know that I know everything."

OUT OF THE LOOP

Noting the North trial's difficulties in finding jurors who don't know anything about Iran-Contra, comedian Johnny Carson says the only one who qualifies so far is Bush.

••••••••••••••••••••

HEADLINE: Democratic presidential candidate Senator Gary Hart drops out after alleged affair

••••••••••••••••••••

DOMESTIC AFFAIRS

Some Capitol Hill wags suggest that Gary Hart's new slogan will be "Win one for the zipper."

••••••••••••••••••••

COLD WAR

The new slogan for Hart's wife would be "Trust, but verify."

TYPE CAST

House Majority Leader Jim Wright, asked to state a broad rule for hiring secretaries and avoiding congressional sex scandals, responded: "The Wright broad rule is that broads ought to be able to type."

•••••••••••••••••••••

HISTORICAL FOOTNOTE: The Watergate scandal is named after a break-in at Democratic headquarters at the Watergate office building in an apparent attempt to plant bugging devices during the 1972 presidential campaign of George McGovern. A subsequent White House cover-up and the release of secretly recorded White House tapes—with "expletives deleted" in transcripts—led to the resignation of President Richard Nixon on August 9, 1974.

•••••••••••••••••••••

NOW HEAR THIS

Mark Russell says that Democratic presidential candidate "George McGovern knew something was up when he picked up a grapefruit and got a dial tone."

HOT STUFF

A 1972 White House memo on anti-McGovern sabotage carried this instruction: "Please burn before reading."

••••••••••••••••••••••

INSIDE JOB

Nixon impressionist David Frye declares, "My administration has taken crime out of the streets and put in the White House where I can watch it."

••••••••••••••••••••••

WATERGATE JOKERS

Washington jesters now refer to President Nixon as "an impeachable White House source."

••••••••••••••••••••••

BIBLICAL PROPORTIONS

The Reverend Billy Graham's Bible reading at the White House now extends from Revelations through the Exodus.

I AM NOT A QUITTER!

Why did Nixon give a speech on the energy crisis? Because he lost his resignation speech.

••••••••••••••••••••

SMOKING BUMPER

A new bumper sticker appears in Washington: "Impeach the (expletive deleted)."

••••••••••••••••••••

THIRD-RATE DESCRIPTION

Presidential press secretary Ron Ziegler's term for news stories the White House doesn't like: "Out-of-context partisan-involved leakage."

••••••••••••••••••••

PARDON ME

A postresignation joke: Nixon said to Ford, "I beg your pardon. The one you promised me in the Rose Garden."

CHAPTER NINE

It's the Stupid Economy

IN GREENSPAN WE TRUST

A lecture by University of Texas Professor James Galbraith on economic growth and the Federal Reserve is entitled: "Who Made Alan Greenspan God Anyway?"

• •

WE WILL BURY—US?

Treasury Secretary Robert Rubin in a speech on the American record in international affairs inadvertently boasted of "the defeat of capitalism."

• •

CHAIRWOMAN IN WAITING

Clinton budget chief Alice Rivlin, introduced at a dinner as patiently awaiting confirmation to be Fed vice chairwoman, interrupts to say, "Oh, not that patiently."

CLOUDED CRYSTAL BALL?

Federal Reserve Chairman Alan Greenspan informs lawmakers that "fundamentally, the future is unknowable."

•••••••••••••••••••••

BIG MUDDY

Asked to remind a Senate committee of his position on an issue, Fed chief Greenspan replied: "I think you have me on the record as being ambiguous on that question."

•••••••••••••••••••••

CAREFUL DEPARTURE

Economist Jeremy Gluck predicts Greenspan's tombstone will read: "I am guardedly optimistic about the next world, but remain cognizant of the downside risks."

CURVE BALL

Eavesdroppers at a party were briefly stunned to hear Federal Reserve Board Chairman Alan Greenspan pronounce it a "terrible week"; but instead of the economy, he was talking about a Baltimore Orioles losing streak.

••••••••••••••••••••

THIN ICE

Economist Edward Yardeni accuses the Fed of "the Tonya Harding approach to monetary policy: clubbing the economy in the knees just because it is performing well."

••••••••••••••••••••

NO EXIT

Treasury Secretary Robert Rubin celebrates a Passover seder on an Air Force plane headed to Bali for a finance ministers meeting. One ritual is dropped: opening the door to let in the prophet Elijah.

FORECASTER'S DIET

One economic forecaster cautions: "He who lives by the crystal ball must soon learn to eat ground glass."

• •

IVORY TOWER

Senator Fritz Hollings of South Carolina defines an economist as "someone who finds something in practice and wonders if it would work in theory."

• •

EXHIBIT A

The title of a paper delivered at an American Economics Association meeting: "Stylometrics: Statistical Evidence on the Decline in the Quality of Writing in the Economics Profession."

THE BRIGHT SIDE

After talk of impeaching Treasury Secretary Robert Rubin over his debt-limit moves prompts a drop in financial markets, one top government official notes: "Could have been worse. The market could have gone up."

•••••••••••••••••••••

GUESS WHO'S BUYING LUNCH

After a White House aide mentions balancing the family budget in talks on the balanced-budget amendment, multimillionaire Treasury Secretary Robert Rubin quips: "I don't know about the rest of you, but I run a surplus."

•••••••••••••••••••••

HIDDEN ASSETS

After reading an erroneous report putting his wealth at $70 million, Treasury Secretary Lloyd Bentsen's wife asks: "Where is it?"

SERIOUS MONEY

Federal Reserve Vice Chairman Alan Blinder says that "a little stodginess" at the central bank is entirely appropriate.

••••••••••••••••••••

MONEY TALKS

Former Housing Secretary Kemp, poking fun at himself, quips, "What follows a Jack Kemp speech about currency? Another Jack Kemp speech about currency."

••••••••••••••••••••

PRUDENT POLICY

Clinton economist Joseph Stiglitz says his view on the dollar's strength is guided by one rule: "I never disagree with the secretary of the treasury."

••••••••••••••••••••

BEAR MARKET

Pittsburgh economist Stuart Hoffman derides the administration's "Goldilocks scenario"—an economy that is not too hot, not too cold, but just right.

HUH?

The U.S. Chamber of Commerce says the latest increase in the U.S. trade deficit "is not as bad as it seems and is more than meets the eye."

••••••••••••••••••••

SEEING RED

The House Democratic Study Group corrects an error in a budget fact sheet to read "surplus," not "deficit." It says, "Our only explanation for this error is force of habit."

••••••••••••••••••••

VOODOO ECONOMICS

Federal Reserve Chairman Paul Volcker says economists and arthritis doctors have something in common: "We still find our patients and clients, with distressing frequency, seeking relief by turning to today's equivalent of snake oil and witchcraft."

PICK 'EM

Asked by a lawmaker whether interest rates will "go up, down, or stay the same?" Fed Chairman Volcker boldly predicts: "One of those."

•••••••••••••••••••••

HOLY MOSES!

With Federal Reserve Chairman Paul Volcker's term expiring next year, an international banker cracks: "Even if they replace him with God, the markets will go down."

•••••••••••••••••••••

MILLER TIME

Reagan administration budget director James Miller boasts that his tough budgeteers are "the kind of people that run over dogs," adding; "I meant that in the best possible way."

BLUEGRASS ECONOMICS

According to transcripts of 1987 Fed meetings, then New York Fed President Gerry Corrigan based his concerns about the economy on "Kentucky windage," meaning, "You throw a piece of grass up, and you see which way it blows."

•••••••••••••••••••••

NEWT IS MY SHEPHERD

Princeton economist Alan Blinder suggests a constitutional amendment requiring school children to pray for a balanced budget.

•••••••••••••••••••••

POLICY POOPERS

Federal Reserve Chairman G. William Miller describes the duty of monetary–policy makers as "taking away the punch just when the party is getting good."

CONSPIRACY THEORY

Economist Herbert Stein says his new book, an inside view of Nixon economic policies, "will soon be in your neighborhood theaters as Oliver Stone's *The Keynesian Nixon.*"

••••••••••••••••••••••

CALL THE DOCTOR

Bush administration deputy Treasury secretary John Robson warns that "the cancer of overregulation is gnawing at America's economic entrails."

••••••••••••••••••••••

LOOKING GOOD

One Washington wag says the highest ranking woman in the Reagan administration is Rosy Scenario.

THE DEVIL YOU SAY

One Reagan regulator opposing bailouts of sick thrift institutions remarks, "Capitalism without failure is like Christianity without Hell."

• • • • • • • • • • • • • • • • • • • •

BAKER'S DOZEN

Reagan White House chief of staff Donald Regan inscribes a photo to James Baker, his successor as Treasury secretary: "It's really an easy job—assets are on the left, liabilities on the right, and they must balance."

• • • • • • • • • • • • • • • • • • • •

NOT AGAIN!

Responding to supply siders' call for reduced capital gains taxes, Dukakis economic adviser Lawrence Summers quips: "I feel a sense of déjà voodoo."

ON THE OTHER HAND

Ronald Reagan says there is a new version of Trivial Pursuit for economists: "In this one there are 100 questions—3,000 answers."

••••••••••••••••••••

MICKEY MOUSE ECONOMICS

President Carter, speaking at Disney World, said he looked forward to seeing Fantasy Land "because it is the source of inspiration for my economic advisers."

CHAPTER TEN

Foreign Entanglements

STOP ME BEFORE I VOTE AGAIN

An Algerian diplomat, explaining his country's recent crackdown, says, "We had to suspend elections to save democracy."

••••••••••••••••••••

ICE COLD

Under fire from business for his tough stance on China trade and human rights, the State Department's Winston Lord tells the U.S. Chamber of Commerce: "I feel a little bit like Tonya Harding joining a Nancy Kerrigan family reunion here."

••••••••••••••••••••

YOU MEAN IT ISN'T?

A Middle East consultant, piqued by his clients' ignorance of the region, begins his briefings by saying, "Iraq isn't the past tense of Iran."

BUG SPRAY

A Washington flower shop advertises "We have more plants than the CIA."

••••••••••••••••••••

CHEAP SKIES

Deputy U.S. Trade Representative Jeff Lang, after flying economy to Geneva for telecommunications talks, says that at his agency, "our idea of luxury is an exit-row seat."

••••••••••••••••••••

WHO CARES?

Damning the Conventional Forces in Europe treaty with the faintest of praise, Senator Jesse Helms of North Carolina declares, "I would get angry about this treaty if it meant anything."

BETWEEN IRAQ AND A HARD PLACE

Jay Leno, noting that President Bush had frozen Iraqi assets, suggests a tougher move: "How about putting all their assets in a savings and loan?"

••••••••••••••••••••••

BETWEEN IRAQ AND A SOFT PLACE

The good news is Saddam Hussein will be tried for war crimes. The bad news is the case will be heard by the Senate Ethics Committee.

••••••••••••••••••••••

RING-A-DING-DING

Comic Argus Hamilton says the United States is still trying to drive Saddam Hussein nuts: "Just today, his wife received a dozen red roses signed, 'You were wonderful last night. Love, Frank Sinatra.'"

STRAIGHT TALK

Bush administration diplo-jargon: "scenario-dependent post-crisis strategy." *Translation:* We'll figure out what to do when the war's over.

••••••••••••••••••••••

IRAQ ATTACK

Jokes about Iran's Republican Guard sweep Washington: They were so disorganized they should be renamed "the Democratic Guard."

••••••••••••••••••••••

BY GEORGE

Postwar humor: Baghdad has been renamed: It's now called Bush Gardens.

FAILED SOVIET COUP

Soviet Putsch-plotters, Comedian Yakov Smirnov says, had a strange new disease: "Russian flu—first you get cold feet, then your backbone dissolves."

• •

BREAKING OUT

One irreverent idea for naming the young commonwealth of former Soviet republics: ACNE, for Association of Countries with No Economies.

• •

LOUISIANA BORIS

A Soviet official describes populist figure Boris Yeltsin as "the Huey Long of Soviet politics."

UNDER THE RADAR

General Alexander Haig jokingly tells friends that foreign policy is like the Stealth bomber: You can't see it, but it still works.

•••••••••••••••••••••

SLOW DAY

Asked whether President Bush has "anything significant" on his schedule, spokesman Marlin Fitzwater says: "No, he has a meeting with Henry Kissinger."

•••••••••••••••••••••

POOR ME

Parrying criticism that the World Bank is against the poor, the bank's new president, multimillionaire James Wolfensohn, says, "The only person I've made poor so far by coming to the bank is me."

IT'S A MIDEASTERN

A joke is that at the Camp David peace summit with Israel's Menecham Begin and Egypt's Anwar Sadat, President Carter will cater to Sadat's love of cowboy films by showing the movie *How the West Bank Was Won.*

•••••••••••••••••••••

GRITS AND LOX

Before Israeli Prime Minister Begin left Washington, President Carter gave him a plaque reading "Shalom, Y'all."

•••••••••••••••••••••

APPARENTLY NOT

Henry Kissinger, asked if it is harder to conduct diplomatic negotiations in an election year, replied: "My megalomania, of course, reaches levels in which an admission of inadequacy is next to inconceivable."

INDEX

ABOUT THE AUTHOR

Ronald G. Shafer is the political features editor in the Washington bureau of the *Wall Street Journal*. He joined the *Journal*'s Chicago bureau in 1963 as a reporter and in 1964 moved to the paper's Detroit bureau. In 1968, he joined the Journal's Washington bureau, where he was named a features editor in 1977. He has written frequently on political humor, focusing on subjects ranging from Art Buchwald and Mark Russell to Dan Quayle. He has been the cowriter of the *Journal*'s page-one Washington Wire column since late 1984 and the primary writer since 1994.

Shafer, a native of Columbus, Ohio, is a 1962 graduate of Ohio State University, where he was editor in chief of the campus newspaper, the *Lantern*. He is the coauthor of several books, including *The Complete Book of Home Buying* with Michael Sumichrast. He lives in McLean, Virginia, with his daughter, Kathryn.